National Peanut Day Recipes

Many Delicious Recipes To Celebrate Holiday

Copyright © 2020

All rights reserved.

DEDICATION

The author and publisher have provided this e-book to you for your personal use only. You may not make this e-book publicly available in any way. Copyright infringement is against the law. If you believe the copy of this e-book you are reading infringes on the author's copyright, please notify the publisher at: https://us.macmillan.com/piracy

Contents

Homemade Peanut Butter 1

Peanut Noodles with Mixed Vegetables and Peanut Sauce 7

Peanut Sauce Baked Tofu 12

Vegan Peanut Butter Choc Chip Protein Bars 17

Microwave Chocolate Peanut Butter & Oat Snack Bars 19

No Bake Peanut Butter Biscoff Cookie Dough Bites 24

Peanut Butter Chocolate Chip Cookie Dough Bites 30

Peanut Butter and Jelly Thumbprint Cookies 34

Egg-In-a-Nest Stuffed Peanut Butter Cookie Dough Bites 39

Pretzel Peanut Caramel Peanut Butter Cookie Dough Truffles 43

Vegan Peanut Butter Banana Bread (Gluten/Soy-Free) 50

Homemade Peanut Butter

Homemade Peanut Butter Ingredients

For this peanut butter recipe, you'll need a 16-ounce bag or jar of peanuts. You can use honey roasted, plain, salted, unsalted, or even a jar of mixed nuts. You won't need oil or salt, just peanuts.

How to Make Homemade Peanut Butter

Making peanut butter from scratch takes less than 5 minutes. Simply add peanuts to the canister of the food processor, turn it on and watch it go.

The peanuts go through various stages in the five minutes it takes to go from peanuts to peanut butter: crushed peanuts, peanuts crushed into a fine powder, a paste, a thicker paste, and then a big peanut butter "dough ball" will form.

And just like that, the big ball will magically break down and turn into a gritty peanut butter. Keep processing and the peanut butter will get smoother, creamier, and thin out.

No oil was ever added at any point during processing — just the natural oils from the peanuts are being released.

Keep processing until you're certain the peanut butter is smooth enough for your liking, another minute or so.

Peanut Noodles with Mixed Vegetables and Peanut Sauce

Peanut sauce is so easy and inexpensive to make at home. Just whisk it together in minutes, pour over your favorite noodles and vegetables, and you have an easy, flavorful, healthy meal in less than 15 minutes. No need for takeout when you can make your own peanut noodles in no time. The peanut sauce portion of the recipe can be doubled. Use half for the noodles and save the other half to be used as a vegetable dip, salad dressing, or marinade. Peanut sauce will keep for at least 1 week in an airtight container in the refrigerator.

INGREDIENTS

Peanut Noodles with Mixed Vegetables

2 1/2 to 3 cups thin rice noodles

1/2 cup carrots, roughly sliced

1/2 cup red bell peppers, roughly sliced

1/2 cup broccoli florets

1/2 cup cherry tomatoes

1/3 cup peanuts

1/2 cup+ other vegetables, optional (baby corn, corn, water chestnuts, peas, sugar snap peas, peapods, scallions, green beans, asparagus)

1 cup diced protein, optional (tofu, tempeh, chicken, shrimp, pork, beef)

Peanut Sauce

1/4 cup creamy peanut butter or homemade peanut butter

1/4 cup sesame oil

1/4 cup agave nectar or honey

1 1/2 tablespoons apple cider vinegar, (apple cider or rice wine preferred, regular vinegar, orange juice, or lemon juice may be substituted)

dash soy sauce, optional and to taste

3/4 teaspoon ground ginger

salt and pepper, optional and to taste

pinch cayenne pepper or chili powder, optional and to taste

INSTRUCTIONS

Peanut Noodles with Mixed Vegetables – Place rice noodles in a large microwave-safe bowl, add about 1/4 cup water, and cook on high powder until tender, about 1 1/2 to 2 minutes or until soft; or cook according to package directions.

National Peanut Day Recipes

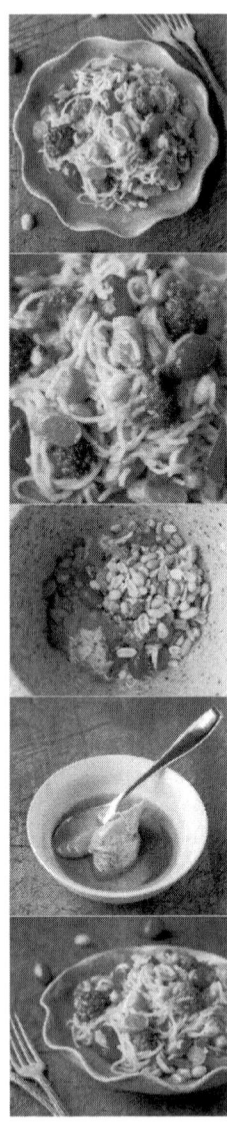

Add the carrots, red peppers, broccoli, cherry tomatoes, peanuts, optional vegetables and protein; set bowl aside.

Peanut Sauce – In a small bowl, combine all ingredients for the peanut sauce and stir or whisk until smooth. Taste sauce and make flavor adjustments if desired.

Pour sauce over noodles and vegetables and toss to coat evenly. Serve immediately; or cover the bowl, refrigerate, and serve chilled. Store leftovers in an airtight container in the refrigerator for up to 3 days and serve chilled or reheat gently in the microwave before serving.

Peanut Sauce Baked Tofu

1 package tofu, pressed (select firm or extra firm)

1/3 c orange juice

3 tbsp peanut butter

3 tbsp sesame oil

3 tbsp agave (or honey/maple syrup or combo)

1 tsp ground ginger

Pinch of cayenne (more to taste, if desired)

Pinch of chili powder (more to taste, if desired)

Optional: 1 Tbsp EVOO or use more sesame oil

Directions:

Pressing your tofu (use a tofu press or press between heavy plates/objects and get the paper towels handy), and slice pressed tofu into 1/4 inch strips.

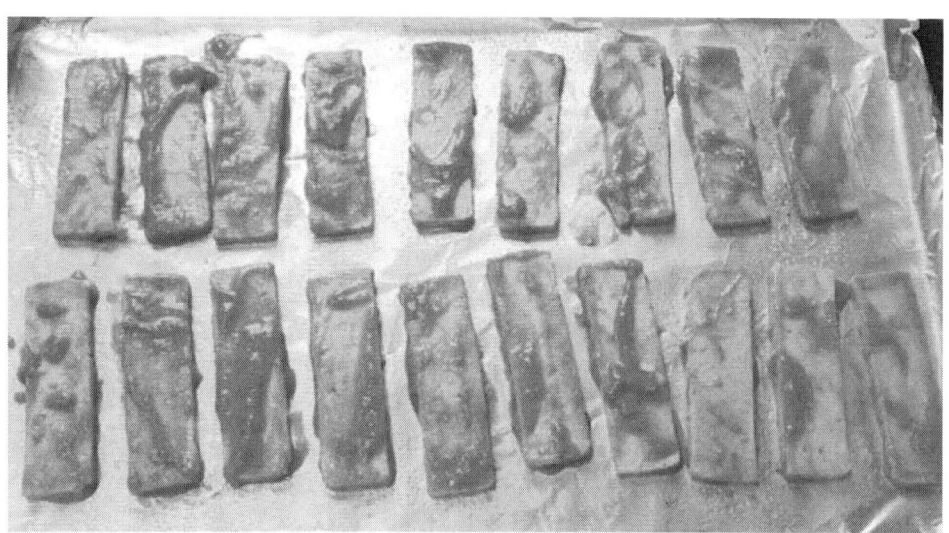

Whisk all marinade ingredients together in a bowl (it will not be pretty) and allow tofu to marinate for at least 20 minutes but a few hours or overnight is ideal. The longer the better. Reserve a couple tablespoons of the marinade that's likely at the bottom of the bowl.

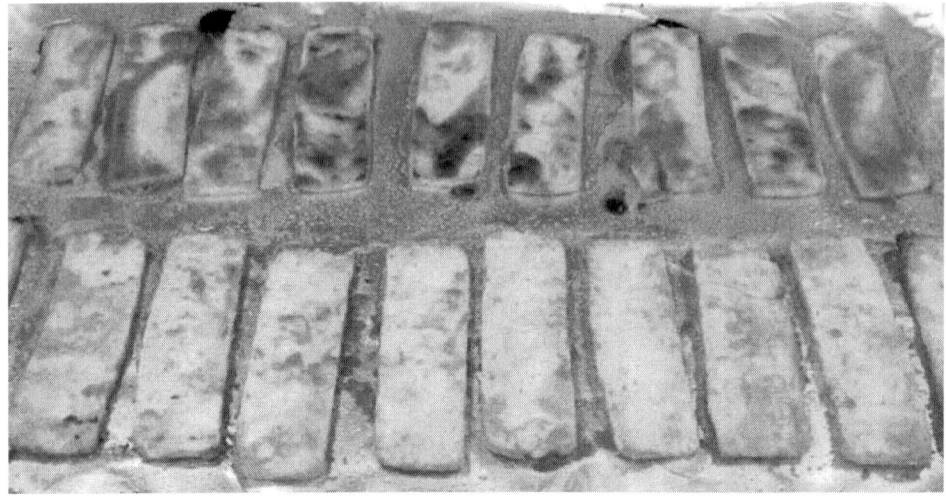

Line a cookie sheet with foil to save on cleanup time and spray with cooking spray.

Broil the marinated tofu for 5-6 minutes on the first side.

Flip, and broil for another 3 to 5 minutes on the second side. Apply what's remaining of the reserved marinade to the top side of the flipped tofu.

Peanut butter + agave can and will go from not done to charred and disgusting in 90 seconds flat. You need to be right there so all your work does not go up in flames and char. Do Not Leave the Kitchen, not even for a second.

Refrigerate leftovers for many days.

Yield: I got 19 strips out of my 1 block of pressed tofu

Vegan Peanut Butter Choc Chip Protein Bars

Ingredients

1 Ripe Banana (mashed)

1.5 c Oats

1/2 c Shredded Coconut (I used sweetened)

1/2 c Raisins (or date chunks, cranberries, craisins, dried cherries/mangoes/apricots/etc. Any dried fruit will work)

1/2 c Chocolate Chips (or carob, butterscotch, white chocolate chips, etc.)

1/2 c Maple Syrup (or agave, yacon syrup)

1/2 c Peanut Butter (or any nut butter, i.e. almond, pecan, cashew, etc.)

The Following Ingredients

2 to 4 scoops of Protein Powder

2 Tbsp Flax Seeds

2 Tbsp Chia Seeds

1.5 Tsp Cinnamon

1 Tsp Vanilla Extract

Yields: Approximately 10 decent sized bars

Note: The above are rough measurements and you can use the kitchen sink mentality on this recipe: a dash of this, a dab of that, don't have this but have tons of that, throw everything in but the kitchen sink strategy and they will "work".

Microwave Chocolate Peanut Butter & Oat Snack Bars

2 Tbsp Chocolate Chips

2 to 3 Tbsp Peanut Butter (or other nut butter)

2 Tbsp Milk (or nut milk) (I used vanilla coffee creamer!)

1/2 C Oats

Optional:

1 Tsp Vanilla Extract

1 Tbsp Sweetener (Brown/White Sugar, Agave, Maple Syrup or Stevia to Taste)

1 Tbsp Other Dry Ingredients (coconut flakes, chia seeds, sunflower seeds, nuts, more chocolate chips, raisins, scoop of protein powder, etc.)

Directions:

National Peanut Day Recipes

Melt the first three ingredients together in the microwave in 30 second intervals, stirring and checking

Then add the Oats and any optional ingredients, stir to combine. (You want this mixture to be fairly dry. If it's not dry enough, add more oats one tablespoon at a time)

Press mixture into bars or balls. Using a piece of plastic wrap on the inside of a square plastic container will save on dishes and cleanup.

Put in refrigerator or freezer for 10 minutes, or until bars have set up. Slice or break apart.

Yields 3 Larabar-sized bars that are also vegan and gluten-free.

No Bake Peanut Butter Biscoff Cookie Dough Bites

1/3 c cashews (unsalted, and raw if possible)

National Peanut Day Recipes

1/3 c oats (whole rolled oats, not quick cook)

1/3 c Biscoff Cookies (or graham crackers or ginger snaps)

2 tbsp brown sugar

1/4 c peanut butter

2 tbsp agave or maple syrup (or combination)

1 tsp vanilla extract

1/4 to 1/3 c chocolate chips

Yields: approximately 16-18 bites

National Peanut Day Recipes

Directions: Add cashews, oats, and Biscoffs to Vita-Mix or food processor and grind into a fine powder.

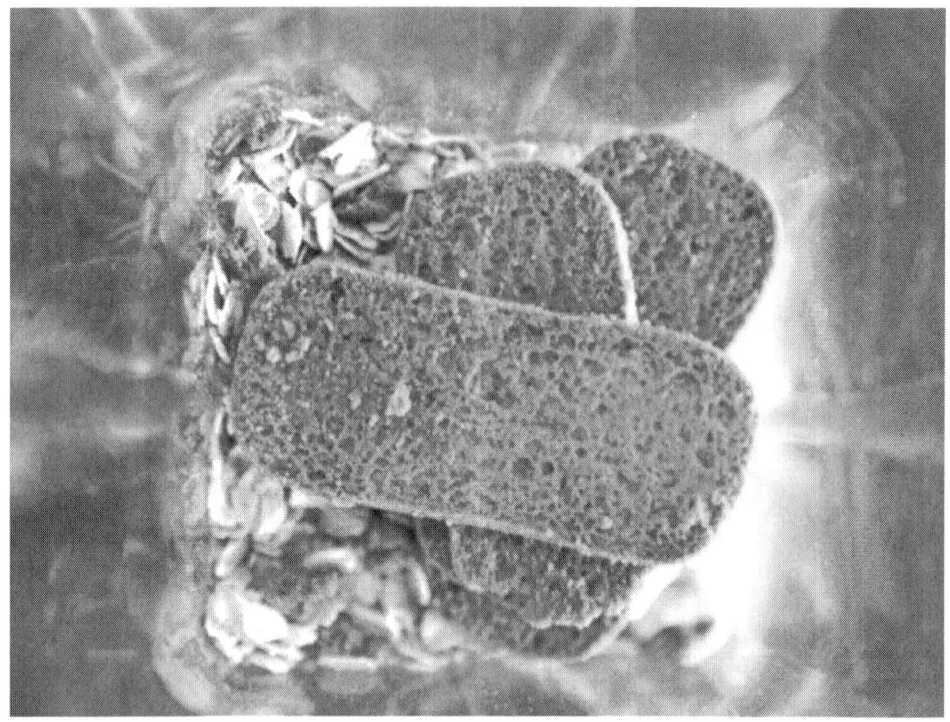

 Then, add brown sugar, peanut butter, agave, and vanilla extract, and blend again. Remove dough from Vita and place into a bowl. Add chocolate chips and stir them in by hand. Roll balls by hand and place in refrigerator or freezer for storage. Will keep for week(s)/month(s) in the freezer.

Notes:

If you don't have Biscoff cookies, use graham crackers or ginger snap cookies

To make this entire recipe Gluten Free, use:

GF graham crackers such as these

Or

Use 1/3 c cashews + 2/3 c oats and omit the Biscoff/Graham crackers entirely

Tips:

If dough is soft or difficult to work with, refrigerate/freeze for 20 minutes prior to forming into balls.

If the dough is too dry, add more peanut butter or agave, a small drizzle at a time.

If the dough is too wet, add more brown sugar or more dry ingredients, i.e. crush another Biscoff or graham cracker and stir it in

Peanut Butter Chocolate Chip Cookie Dough Bites

Makes 20 small balls, 16 medium, or 12 larger

National Peanut Day Recipes

1/4 cup peanut butter

1/8 cup butter, softened (2 tablespoons)

1/4 cup brown sugar

1 tablespoon white sugar

1/2 teaspoon vanilla extract

1/4 cup whole rolled old-fashioned oats (quick cook is probably fine)

1/4 cup all-purpose flour (use a gluten free flour blend of your choice if keeping gluten free; or grind oats and use exclusively oat flour)

pinch salt, optional

1/4 cup mini chocolate chips (or regular size chips are fine)

2 tablespoons chocolate chips or baking chocolate bar, melted for final drizzle

In a small bowl, whip the peanut butter and butter until creamy. Add the sugars and whip until creamy. Add the vanilla extract, salt, oats, flour (add the flour slowly in case you need slightly less than recipe indicates) and stir until just combined.

The dough should be easy to work with and form into balls at this point, but if the dough is too dry or crumbly and not coming together, add a touch more peanut butter until desired consistency is achieved. Conversely, it dough is too wet or sticky, add slightly more oats or flour. Also, chilling the dough in the freezer or refrigerator for 20 minutes prior to shaping it into balls can be helpful if the dough is a little wet or sticky.

After appropriate dough consistency is reached, fold in the chocolate chips and then roll the dough into ball shapes.

Store extras in the refrigerator for weeks or in the freezer for many months.

Peanut Butter and Jelly Thumbprint Cookies

Makes 10 to 12 smaller cookies, or 6 to 8 larger cookies

1/4 cup peanut butter (I used store-brand, inexpensive, non-"natural", creamy peanut butter*)

1/8 cup butter, softened (2 tablespoons) – or margarine, Earth Balance, or similar if keeping vegan

1/4 cup brown sugar

1 tablespoon white sugar

1/4 cup powdered sugar

1/4 teaspoon cinnamon

1 teaspoon vanilla extract

1/4 cup all-purpose flour (to make gluten free, use a gluten free flour blend of your choice such almond/oat/peanut/rice flour)

pinch salt, optional

1/4 cup jelly, or to taste

In a small bowl, whip the peanut butter and butter until creamy. Tip: microwave the peanut butter and butter in a microwave-safe bowl for 15 seconds, taking care not to melt them but just soften them, and they will combine easier. Add the sugars and whip until smooth. Add the cinnamon, vanilla extract, salt, flour (add the flour slowly in case you need slightly less than recipe indicates) and stir until combined.

The dough should be easy to work with and form into balls at this point, but if the dough is dry or crumbly and is not coming together, add a touch more peanut butter and mix until desired consistency is achieved. Conversely, it dough is too wet or sticky, add slightly more flour. Also, chilling the dough in the freezer for 10 minutes or refrigerator for 20-30 minutes prior to shaping it into balls can be helpful if the dough is a little wet or sticky.

After appropriate dough consistency is reached, roll the dough into 1 inch golf ball-sized shapes. After the balls are rolled, indent the tops with your thumb, making a well for the jelly. Treat the dough like clay and form the shapes and sides as you see fit. Then full each well with approximately 1 to 1.5 teaspoons of jelly.

Store extras in the refrigerator for weeks or in the freezer for up to 3 months for longer term storage.

Notes:.

Peanut butter that separates into a solid and oil is not recommended for these cookies.

Raw cookie dough, particularly of the peanut butter variety, is always welcome. The thumbprint peanut butter dough is some of my favorite to date.

It's sweet, full of robust peanut butter flavor, and the vanilla flavor is pronounced.

Egg-In-a-Nest Stuffed Peanut Butter Cookie Dough Bites

Makes 12 to 14 small cookie nests

National Peanut Day Recipes

1/4 cup peanut butter (I used store-brand, inexpensive, non-"natural", creamy peanut butter*)

1/8 cup butter or margarine, softened (2 tablespoons)

1/4 cup brown sugar

1 tablespoon white sugar

1/4 cup powdered sugar

1/4 teaspoon cinnamon

1 teaspoon vanilla extract

1/4 cup all-purpose flour (to make gluten free, use a gluten free flour blend of your choice)

pinch salt, optional

1/4 cup pastel Jordan Almonds (or use plain almonds, peanuts, macadamia nuts, Peanut M&Ms, Whoppers, ball-shaped candy, diced candy bar pieces)

In a small bowl, whip the peanut butter and butter until creamy. Tip: microwave the peanut butter and butter in a microwave-safe bowl for 15 seconds, taking care not to melt them but just soften them, and they will combine easier. Add the sugars and whip until smooth. Add the cinnamon, vanilla extract, salt, flour (add the flour slowly in case you need slightly less than recipe indicates) and stir until combined.

The dough should be easy to work with and form into balls at this point, but if the dough is dry or crumbly and is not coming together, add a touch more peanut butter and mix until desired consistency is achieved. Conversely, it dough is too wet or sticky, add slightly more flour. Also, chilling the dough in the freezer for 10 minutes or refrigerator for 20-30 minutes prior to shaping it into balls can be helpful if the dough is a little wet or sticky.

After appropriate dough consistency is reached, roll the dough into 1 inch golf ball-sized shapes. After the balls are rolled, gently push in and insert an almond or candy. Treat the dough like clay and form the shapes and sides as you see fit. Store extras in the refrigerator for weeks, or in the freezer for up to 3 months for longer term storage.

Notes: I recommend using non-natural peanut butter. Something like Jif, Skippy, or similar. Peanut butter that separates into a solid and oil is not recommended for these cookies. You could likely make these with almond butter, cookie butter, cashew butter, sunflower seed butter, or alternate nut butter or spread but you may need to play around with the ratio of dry ingredients (increase them) since most other nut butters tend to be runnier than peanut butter and you will need more dry ingredients in order to get the dough to come together.

Pretzel Peanut Caramel Peanut Butter Cookie Dough Truffles

Makes 1 dozen (I made 13 from this recipe)

1/4 cup peanut butter

1 tablespoon caramel sauce (try Dark Rum Caramel Sauce or any store-bought jarred caramel sauce or ice cream topping caramel sauce; substitute maple syrup)

2 tablespoons powdered sugar

1 tablespoon brown sugar

1/4 cup pretzels, crushed

1/4 cup peanuts, crushed

Pinch salt, optional to taste

3/4 cup + chocolate chips, melted for dipping

2 tablespoons pretzels and peanut mixture, crushed for garnishing optional

Peanut butter and/or caramel sauce drizzled over the top for garnishing, optional

Combine peanut butter, caramel sauce, and sugars in a small bowl and stir until combined. Add the crushed pretzels and peanuts. Add the dry mixture to the wet mixture and fold to combine.

Roll the dough into small balls, no larger than 1/2 inch in diameter, and place them on a parchment-lined or wax-paper lined flat surface. Tip: Do not roll the balls larger than 1/2 inch in diameter because they become much larger after you coated in chocolate, appearing to nearly double in size. This is a truffle (one bite), not an apricot. Roll smaller than you think and if the dough is difficult to work with, chilling it in the freezer for 15 minutes may be helpful.

Place the rolled cookie dough balls in the freezer for at least a half hour; the colder the better for the next step: dipping.

You could do this over a double boiler if desired.

National Peanut Day Recipes

After the chocolate has melted, removed the chilled cookie dough balls from the freezer and place one ball into the bowl and toss it lightly with two forks in the chocolate bath. Carefully remove the coated ball and set it down on wax or parchment paper. If desired, sprinkle with crushed pretzels before the chocolate fully hardens. Repeat this process with the next 11 balls.

You may need to reheat your chocolate mixture after a few balls, as it will cool down and become more difficult to work with. Reheat in the microwave in 20 to 30 second bursts as needed. After all the balls have been dipped, you can optionally add a drizzle of peanut butter or caramel sauce over the top. Place the finished truffles in the freezer to fully set up for at least 30 minutes before serving.

Store extras in the refrigerator or freezer.

Notes and Tips:

If dough is too wet before rolling into balls, add slightly more dry ingredients (pretzel or peanuts). Or, chilling the dough in the refrigerator or freezer helps, also.

If dough is too dry, add slightly more wet ingredients (peanut butter or caramel sauce).

Vegan Peanut Butter Banana Bread (Gluten/Soy-Free)

3/4 c Oats (that I ground into oat flour)

1 c Almond Flour (or 1 c almonds that you grind)

3 Large Ripe Bananas (Optional: reserve approx 8 little slices for garnishing your loaf or cake)

1 Peeled & Cored Apple (Med to Large)

1 cup creamy peanut butter

1/2 cup White Sugar

1/2 cup Brown Sugar

1 Tbsp Blackstrap Molasses

1 Tsp Baking Soda

1 Tsp Vanilla Extract

tried to blend all those ingredients together.

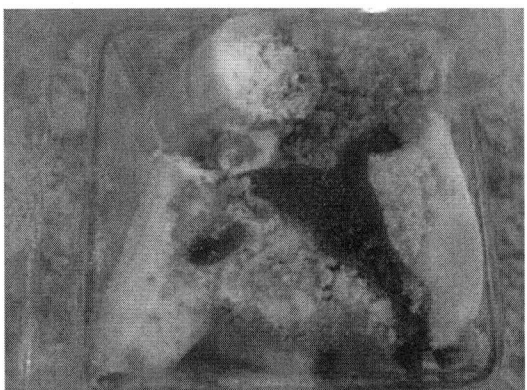

Overhead of ingredients in blender

Wooden spoon showing some of the batter with blender in background

put the Blendtecto rest…

Blender un assembled placed in kitchen drawer

You can imagine that this transfer and the extra cleanup really generated some choice words from my mouth.

Blender showing ingredients being blended

...And the mixture was looking and tasting (finger-licking) good!

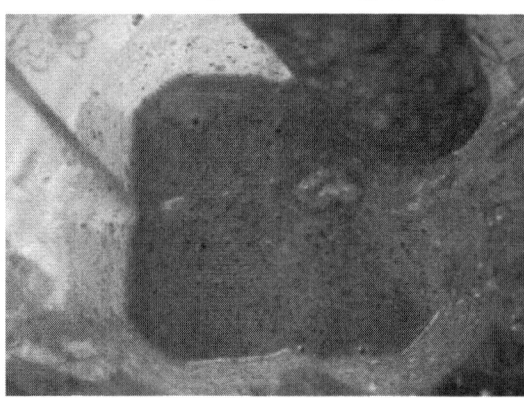

Overhead of blended ingredients in blender

Which just upped the delish factor.

Peanut butter being added to blended ingredients

Blended Again

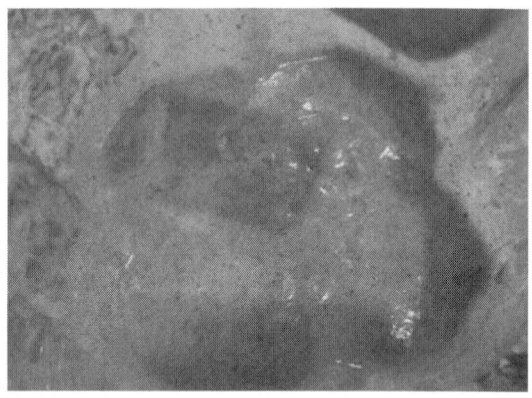

Fully blended mixture in blender

Poured the mixture into a bread pan (9 x 5) **see caveat below. Garnished with a few banana slices. And baked at 325 F in a Convection Oven for 1 hour.

Batter poured into loaf pan and topped with sliced bananas

Finished Peanut Butter Banana Bread taken out of oven

Close up of Peanut Butter Banana Bread showing sliced bananas on top

Here's an up close shot of the finished product. Can you see the ridic amount of moistness this bread has??

Hand holding up a slice of the Vegan Banana Bread

Or try this one on for size

Hand holding slice or bread showing the moistness

If you like really ooey-gooey desserts and are a fan of underbaked treats because you love the moistness, then look no further than this recipe! Plus, it's not overwhelmingly peanut buttery which for some people, is a good thing. If you want it overwhelmingly PB'ish, then just add more PB!

If you're a fan of slightly underbaked treats, no worries, make it in the loaf pan, you'll be in heaven.

Printed in Great Britain
by Amazon